INTERDISCIPLINARY
INTERACTION
DESIGN

INTERDISCIPLINARY
INTERACTION
DESIGN

Quotes

"Interdisciplinary Interaction Design by James Pannafino fills a huge gap in the training of designers. It's concise summary of critical concepts effectively introduces the designer to the most important concepts. This handy book is a must have for anyone that truly wants to make the most of their career as a web designer and will serve as a launching point to many areas that will pop up throughout their career."
- Patrick McNeil, author of the bestselling book series
  The Web Designer's Idea Book(s)

"James has put together a collection of easy to understand and incredibly useful insights into Web design and usability. There's something here for everyone – from basic concepts to advanced theory – uniquely presented in a visual way."
- Brian Miller Ed.D, author of Above the Fold: Understanding
  the Principles of Successful Web Site Design

"An excellent guide to the principals and terminology that anyone new to the interactive discipline will need to know and master over their course of their career ... and also a good refresher to those of us that have been doing it for a bit."
- Todd Miller, Principal and Managing Partner of The Archer Group

"With Interdisciplinary Interaction Design James Pannafino has created a valuable resource for all interaction designers and those interested in learning about the field. I find myself coming back to Interdisciplinary Interaction Design, it's a very helpful reference."
- Tobias Treppmann, Web Designer, andCulture

Read First

All information provided in this book is either based on professional referenced research, personal experience, common knowledge or professional feedback. The author has worked hard to present correct and current information in this book. He cannot assure that all the information will fit every situation or is completely in line with each discipline's perspective.

Copyright © 2012 by James Pannafino
ISBN: 978-0-9826348-1-3
Library of Congress Control Number: 2012920044

www.interdisciplinaryinteractiondesign.com
Published by Assiduous Publishing

Cover Design: Kate Whitecomb

This book is dedicated to all of the great theorists and professionals that made this project possible.

About the Author

James Pannafino is a faculty member at Millersville University, Pennsylvania in the Art and Design Department where he teaches graphic and interactive design courses. Before teaching at the college level, James worked as both a graphic and interactive designer in the professional field. His research interests include Interactive design fundamentals, visualization, visual storytelling and digital narrative forms.

James has presented at conferences at the following institutions and universities: HOW Interactive Design, Fordham University, Harvard University, Maryland Institute of College and Art, Penn State University, and Rensselaer Polytechnic Institute.

His love for communication design and visualization has led him to produce his first book; *Common College Sense: The Visual Guide to Understanding Everyday Tasks for College Students.* The book uses both visual diagrams and written explanations to clearly describe common-sense tasks.

Table of Contents

Acknowledgments

Family and Friends

Their encouragement and belief in me have always meant a lot.
The amount of time it took to research, write, design and publish
a book was time away from them, but I always felt they were there
supporting me.

Professional Experts and Theorists

There are so many intelligent and generous professionals out there
that have written books, articles or have presented their research
that have helped influence the content of this book. Many were kind
enough to comment on this project and give it a recommendation.
Without their work, many pages in this book would not be possible.

Reviewers

Special thanks goes to every person who has added their insight
to this project. From my friends to my colleagues, your feedback
helped make this book what it is today.

You, the Readers

I would like to thank the people that have purchased this book. From
the librarian adding it to a collection, an educator teaching a class
and the people who saw this book worthy of their bookshelves. There
was a lot of hard work put into this project; I hope it fills the needs
you were seeking.

Foreward

I find *Interdisciplinary Interaction Design* to be one sly little book. My colleague, author and designer James Pannafino, takes absolutely nothing for granted in this work: from what can seem at first very simple to the most dauntingly complex. Here we see the vocabulary that has fed into and continues to emerge from within the field of interaction design being held up to the light, shaken free of any hint of (insider) pretension or presumption, and presented to the reader in page after insightful page of eminently deployable couplets of words and images. "Ready-to-hand," as philosopher of technology Martin Heidegger once famously remarked about the ease with which we usually pick up a hammer and put it to work. *Interdisciplinary Interaction Design* delights in the powers of its tool-presentation: collapsing the unnecessary and not-extinct-soon-enough distinction between tools for thought (theories and concepts) and tools for action (machines and systems) into one single aim -- what does this design element do?

It makes sense, of course, that any book focused on sorting through the layers of complexity that inform the design of everyday interfaces as they aspire for seamless accessibility should, in its own manner of its execution, be supremely user-friendly.

I should add that *Interdisciplinary Interaction Design* is, in its endearing matter-of-factness, a subtly funny book too. Its charm lies in its capacity to nudge the reader with one sentiment over again and again: "Put me to work." So, what are you waiting for? Time to get started.

- Gregory J. Seigworth,
  Professor of Communication, Millersville University , PA

Preface

I love learning new terminology, as an educator that is part of what I do; I teach various terms within the context of the educational process. As an interactive design professor, I am responsible for teaching timeless design principles (typography and compositional layout) and interactive technology (capabilities and limitations). Sometimes those timeless design principles don't always align in context with the technology aspects of interactive design. Mastering one aspects is hard enough, but trying to learn both at the same time makes it much more challenging.

As a teacher in a liberal arts university, I must find a balance and supply my students with a foundation of knowledge that will carry them throughout their careers. The more and more I looked at the core principles of interactive design, the more I realized they weren't solely based on traditional design or the technology side. Industrial designers have been dealing with usability factors for ages; the field of communication has plenty of theories in digital media; and cognitive psychology talks to how people process information. True interaction design is best fostered in an interdisciplinary approach.

Various disciplines tap into different sides of our brain. Sometimes the right and left sides don't always work together as smoothly as one might think. However, if we create a visual context with supportive text and examples through clear metaphors, hopefully the information can be understood regardless of the type of learning style. By visualizing timeless interdisciplinary terminology in various contexts, interaction design education can have a foundation to support a liberal arts curriculum and interdisciplinary learning environment.

Introduction

Interactive design tends to be an umbrella term, often used in higher education and industry to encompass multiple disciplines that fall into the interactive realm. Interaction design is one of interactive design's subsets and can be described as the design of digital devices, interfaces and the interaction of the user and said design. Interaction design was coined by Bill Moggridge and further explained and studied by Alan Cooper in his book *About Face 3: The Essentials of Interaction Design.* Interaction design can be seen in various disciplines such as psychology, human computer interaction, user experience, industrial design and many others (Figure 1).

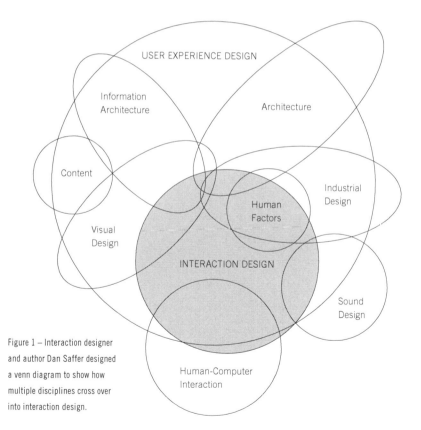

Figure 1 – Interaction designer and author Dan Saffer designed a venn diagram to show how multiple disciplines cross over into interaction design.

Designing for Interaction: Creating Innovative Applications and Devices by Dan Saffer

This book further explores the idea of interaction design across disciplines and the various principles that can help with the application of timeless theories in the interactive design process. It also explores less represented disciplines that relate to interaction design such as comics, gaming, motion design and business, to name a few. It uses visual translation, metaphors and concise explanations to create a guide for users to start to grasp various theories. These concepts explore interaction between humans, computers and information as a whole. This entails how we see and understand words, the meaning of imagery, how space and time affect interaction and human behaviors and how our information and digital devices affect our actions within the world and objects that surround us.

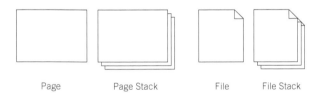

Page   Page Stack   File   File Stack

Figure 2 – User-experience expert Jesse James Garrett created the well-known "Visual vocabulary for describing information architecture and interaction design." Basic units of presentation (left).

Due to the interdisciplinary nature of this project, each discipline can take away its own meaning or usage from the examples in this book. My hope is that this book adds to the basic foundation (Figure 2) of interdisciplinary principles and theories for interaction design thinking across disciplines; that it also continues to create a visual language for the better understanding of complex principles; and that it is a starting point for further exploration of each term's meaning.

All the best,
James Pannafino

Guide to Understanding the Book

This section will help the users understand what each part is for and how to navigate through the information. Each principle is one to two pages in length and has five components to it.

1 Discipline

The top left of each page shows the origin of where the term originates from. In some cases, the term lives in multiple disciplines, or is just based on the referencing material source.

2 Title

This is the actual terminology that is being explored and is displayed at the largest type size. In some cases, multiple terms are presented at the same time due to the related nature and connected meaning of each other.

3 Description

Written in conversational tone for easy accessibility, each description attempts to break down the term to its core idea. In some cases, the description will directly support the visual below it, and in other cases it will work alongside of the visuals and allow the sub-description to further define the supporting context.

4 Visual Representation and Sub-Description

Diagrams, metaphors and comparative imagery are used to visually explain each term and support the written description. Each visual component is further defined by a sub-description that explains the example in more detail. Many Web site/interface examples are represented in basic line form and are generic and devoid of style.

DISCIPLINE: WEB DESIGN

Page Fold

In Web design there is an imaginary line that creates a fold or separation of content on the page before scrolling is started. The content that is seen by the viewer is known as "above the fold" and tends to have more importance, whereas content below the fold is given secondary awareness. The term above the fold comes from editorial design where a newspaper's fold generally cuts the front page content in half, forcing the designer to consider what to put on the top half.

Newspaper Page Fold [1]

Digital Design Page Fold

Page Fold

Feature articles, page guides and premier ads tend to appear above the fold on the front page of a newspaper.

In digital design the navigation and feature area needs to appear above the fold. Also, there needs to be a visual cue for the user to scroll to see the content below the fold.

1 Above the Fold: Understanding the Principles of Successful Web Site Design by Brian Miller.

5 Credit / Reference Line

When a particular person has coined a term, he/she is referenced in the description section. If the term is used by multiple experts, but has heavily influenced the description and visualization, they are credited here. All other sources are referenced in the back of the book.

Activating Compositional Space

Activating compositional space is the idea of taking white space and having it create a positive flow with the surrounding content. Simply placing negative space throughout a composition does not always enhance the content and can lead to visual clutter. If applied correctly, activating compositional space will assist in determining hierarchy, visual rest and reading gravity.

Activating Compositional Space

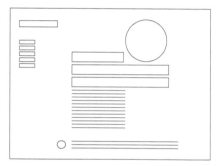

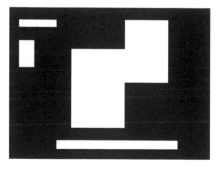

By creating visual rest and allowing reading gravity to happen uninterrupted, the compositional space becomes activated.

Trapped Compositional Space

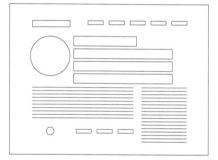

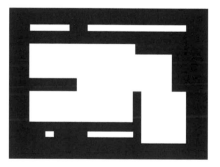

Space around the content is cluttered and trapped, causing it to form gaps in the composition that restrict reading flow.

Affordances

When objects or designs signal properties or functions, the affordance describes to us what they are used for or what they do. A handle on a drawer allows (or affords) us to push and pull the drawer. Similarly, a button on a digital page affords us to press it. If the affordance is used properly, a basic task should be easily utilized. When a basic affordance is too complex and needs more description, then the affordance no longer informs the user about the design's purpose. Also see Signals and Cues.

Physical Affordances

A vertical crossbar on a door affords the user to open the door by pushing.

The handle signals pull, but the function does not afford the user to complete the task; it needs further explanation and fails as a basic design.

The Design of Everyday Things by Donald A. Norman

Digital Affordances

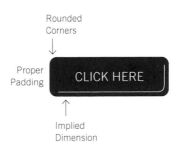

FORM / DIMENSION

Familiar shape and dimension of buttons afford users the ability to click that area to create an interaction. Note: This is just one of many possible examples.

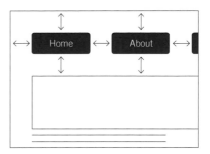

PROXIMITY

Proper spacing between navigational elements and content affords the user the ability to click a button.

Analog and Digital Devices

Analog devices use signals (frequency, current, charge, etc.) to communicate information from one device to another. For example, a simple rotary phone translates the human voice into pulses that travel the phone lines. Digital devices use binary code to send information without generation loss from one device to another where it translates into the intended content. Analog devices have a long history but because of their reproduction degradation, they have limited capabilities and options. Digital devices have multiple capabilities and are often easily compatible with other digital devices.

Analog Signal Waveform

Original Signal ———————————————————— Received Signal

Analog signals use waves or pulses to send information.

Digital Signal Waveform

Original Signal ———————————————————— Received Signal

0001001000100100010001000100100010010001001

Digital signals encode analog signal into binary code.

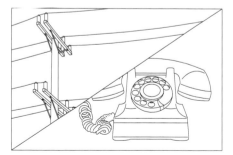

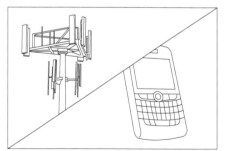

ANALOG

Signal to noise ratio: The waveform is susceptible to electrical interface. Telephone line signal may be affected by the weather or other external noise interference.

DIGITAL

Signal to noise ratio: The waveform is encoded and is unaffected by noise. If the signal is decoded, the waveform will simply drop.

Branching and Nodes

A very basic type of interactive structure often found in early game design involves a basic type of choice between user and interface. Each point of choice is called a node and the path between each is called a branch. While simple to start, direct branching tends to waste unused paths and can grow out of control for long form interactive structures.

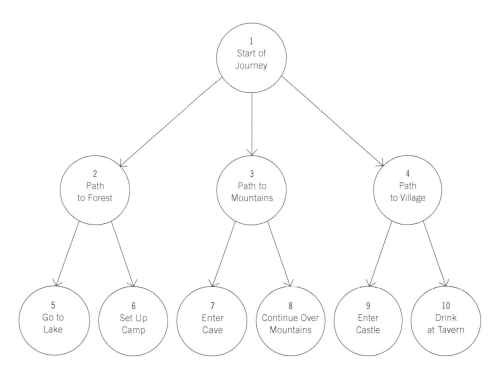

Each node (circles) can continue to
branch (lines with arrows) out to
multiple other nodes and arrows.

Breadcrumb Trail

A breadcrumb trail is a single line of dynamic text or visual links. They show the users the path they have taken, the location of where they are at or the attributes of the information on the page. Breadcrumbs need to act as a secondary navigation aid and should not compete in any way with the primary navigation scheme. Each link can be selected at any time, but it is good practice to use breadcrumbs only when there is more than one page to link together.

Dynamic Text Breadcrumbs

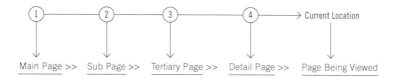

The classic version of breadcrumbs tends to have dynamic text and uses the greater than ">" symbol on the keyboard to separate levels (numbered above) of pages. Example: Location Type, five pages from start.

Graphical Breadcrumbs

Graphic or image-based breadcrumbs may use the combination of symbols and text links to create separations. Example: Attribute Type.

Button Interaction States

The following are three examples of button interaction states. The first is an analog button, which is commonly found on keyboards, alarm clocks and various power buttons. The second is a digital interface button, which is often seen on digital tablets and mobile phones. The last is a standard GUI interface where the user manipulates a mouse or track pad to control an arrow on screen. Also see Affordances and Signals and Cues.

Analog Button Interaction

| The Static state extends up off the interface to physically signal it is a button. | The Clicked/Pressed state is activated when the user presses down on the button. |

Digital Button Interaction

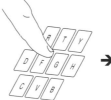 

| While still physically activated by hand, the Static state is flat on most digital devices. | When Clicked/Pressed, the button is activated. In some cases an audible sound is also made. |

Computer Button Interaction States

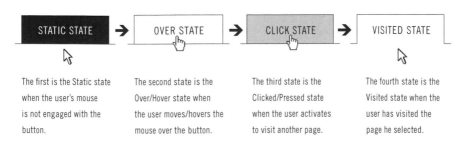

| The first is the Static state when the user's mouse is not engaged with the button. | The second state is the Over/Hover state when the user moves/hovers the mouse over the button. | The third state is the Clicked/Pressed state when the user activates to visit another page. | The fourth state is the Visited state when the user has visited the page he selected. |

Call to Action

A call to action (sometimes called call to action buttons) is simply a visual prompt (call) by the designer to the user in hope of a response (action). They can be used to encourage users to sign up for a service, download specific information or even buy a product. Urgent language that activates the user's attention is often seen in action buttons, such as "Register Now" or "Try it for Free."

Call to Action Button

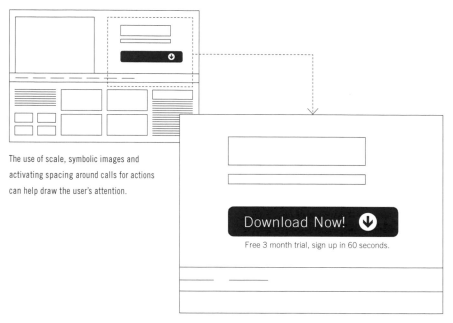

The use of scale, symbolic images and activating spacing around calls for actions can help draw the user's attention.

Content around the "call for action" should support its cause and communicate to the user that the path is worth taking.

Card Sorting

Card sorting is a low-tech technique of organizing navigational systems and creating a folksonomy of information for a Web site or digital experiences. Open card sorting is when the participant has to group content cards into groups based on their associations. Closed card sorting is when organizational groups are pre-established for the participant, where he must place each card into a group.

Each card has a label of a page or content source for the participant to group into similar clusters (open). If it is closed, the clusters are given to the participant beforehand.

Open Card Sorting

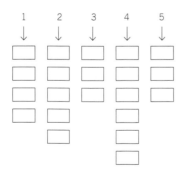

Once the cards are organized into groups, potential categories and structures may be revealed.

Closed Card Sorting

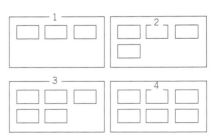

Pre-established groupings allow stakeholders to see how new information works with existing content.

Cartesian Coordinates System

The three-dimensional Cartesian coordinate system depicts three axes that cross each other to help simulate 3D imagery. The X axis controls the horizontal dimensions that reflect the landing plane. The Y axis controls the vertical dimensions that allow the camera to control the viewing plane. The Z axis controls the spatial quality, which reseed and projects within the space plane.

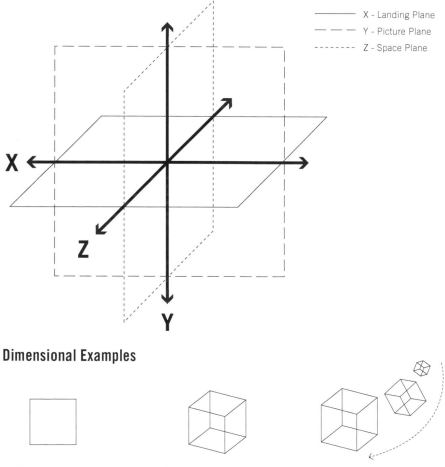

————— X - Landing Plane
— — — Y - Picture Plane
-------- Z - Space Plane

Dimensional Examples

Two-dimensional square uses both the X and Y coordinates.

Three-dimensional square uses both the X , Y and Z coordinates.

Four-dimensional square uses X, Y, Z coordinates and also rotates, scales and moves in space.

Chunking

When writing and designing large amounts of information for a digital experience, it helps to envision the content into topics and subtopics and avoid reflecting a long form document (such as a printed novel). The strategy of chunking information into smaller parts is used to afford users the ability to scan information. There are various ways to chunk information such as writing short paragraphs and sentences, highlighting key phrases or creating bulleted lists. Chunking creates an organized format that helps users predict future sections of the digital page yet to be explored.

Running Paragraph

A long running paragraph has no visual hierarchy and does not have areas for visual rest.

Chunking Information

By creating emphasis on the intro paragraph, using bullets and separating content with visual rest, the user has a proper structure to read from.

Cloud Computing

Cloud computing is the concept of accessing applications and storing file information online. "Cloud" is a metaphor for the Internet due to the way flowchart diagrams have a cloud-like shape drawn around them. The actual files do not exist on the local hard drive, but can be accessed via the cloud. Some cloud based services offer the advantage to share information via network, where there is only one copy of a file in which multiple people can work on at the same time. This is much easier than having multiple versions of one file.

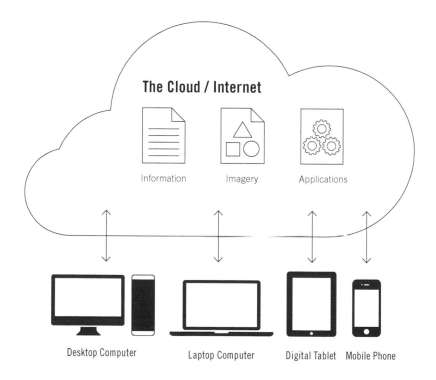

The Cloud / Internet

Information   Imagery   Applications

Desktop Computer   Laptop Computer   Digital Tablet Mobile Phone

Cognitive Load Theory

Cognitive load theory refers to the amount of new information our working memory can hold and the amount of tasks it can process. Long-term memory is something we store and use in a later time. Designers work towards the hope that the user will be able to transfer information from working memory (a designer-created task) to the long term to be recalled later and at a faster pace when revisiting that task. A designer wants to avoid overwhelming the users with too much information, so they don't give up.

Miller's Magic Number 7

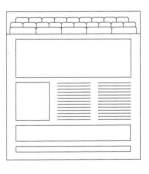

Psychologist George Miller is theory "The Magical Number Seven, Plus or Minus Two" refers to how a person's memory span can only hold around seven objects. A well-designed menu will limit features and break information into sections (left). Similarly a more manageable digital experience might have a limited number of primary navigation links (right).

Information Overload

Author Alvin Toffler discussed "Information Overload" where the senses are overwhelmed, and decisions are stifled because a person is unable to process the information. A menu with too many choices may cause a patron to be indecisive (left). In a digital interface, too many buttons in one nav bar may cause the user to leave the site or choose the wrong link (right).

Content Inventory

A content inventory is the overall process of taking stock of the information on a Web site, where the content audit is the actual tool where all the information is recorded. The process of conducting a content audit consists of clicking through each Web page in the order of the Web site structure. The recording is usually done in a tabulated form program and can have many different types of categories depending on what level of depth the audit is intended for.

Content Audit

Page ID	Page Name	Link Source	Notes
1.0	Home Page	http://www.design.com/index.html	
2.0	About	http://www.design.com/about/	
2.1	History	http://www.design.com/about/history.html	
2.2	Leadership	http://www.design.com/about/leadership.h	
2.3	Giving Back	http://www.design.com/about/giving.html	Broken link on page
3.0	Process	http://www.design.com/process/	
3.1	Research	http://www.design.com/process/research.l	
3.2	Design	http://www.design.com/process/design.ht	
3.3	Testing	http://www.design.com/process/testing.ht	
3.3.1	Application	http://www.design.com/process/testing/ap	
3.3.2	User Testing	http://www.design.com/process/testing/us	
4.0	Work	http://www.design.com/work/	
4.1	Branding	http://www.design.com/work/branding.htn	Update work
4.2	Interactive	http://www.design.com/work/interactive.ht	
5.0	Contact	http://www.design.com/work/contact.html	Change form return

While this content audit consists of Page ID, Page Name, Link Source and Notes, it can also have other categories such as Document Type, Keywords, ROT (Redundant, Outdated or Trivial Information) section and others.

Controls

Controls are common components within screen-based interface design that allow the user to change, adjust or manipulate interface content. Controls can fit into different categories[1] (see below), working either together or separately. While users might be familiar with standard controls, the use of them does not equal good design and should only be used in the right situation. Below are just a few different types of examples of controls.

Action based Controls

Action-based controls can be seen in controls that take a direct action. Buttons and links are examples of action-based controls.

Selection-based Controls

Selection-based controls allow the user to select one or more choices on screen. An example is a list of check boxes; the user can click on and off the box as needed.

Input-based Controls

Input-based controls allow the user to enter information into a bound or unbound field of entry. Spin boxes are an example of both; the arrow buttons form bound increments and the field leaves it open for unbound entry.

Display based Controls

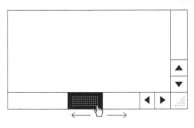

Display-based controls help operate the displays within an interface design. A common example are scrollbars that allow users to access information beyond the portal of viewability.

1 About Face 3: The Essentials of Interaction Design" Alan Cooper, Robert Reimann and David Cronin

Data-Ink Ratio

While visually displaying quantitative information, the ratio of ink[1] (or digital equivalent) should be balanced enough to add substance to the graphic. Using decorative elements with no purpose may lead towards distorting the data or the user misinterpreting the data. While visual elements can enhance a design, too much "junk" is not necessary.

Low Ratio

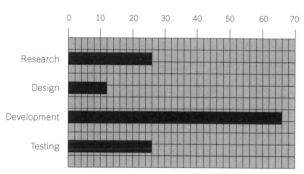

The background tone, graph lines and border are all inessential data-ink. By having multiple visual elements, nothing is allowed to stand out, thus muting the ink ratio.

High Ratio

By deleting the superfluous visual elements (background tone, graph lines and border) there is a clear focus on the data-ink. Thus, the data can more clearly be communicated to the user.

1 Data-Ink Ratio - The Visual Display of Quantitative Information by Edward R. Tufte
Graph Diagrams reference: http://www.tbray.org/ongoing/data-ink/di5

Decision Scale

To create immersive game play, there needs to be enough ups and downs to keep the game interesting yet not overwhelming. In the book *Game Design Workshop* Tracy Fullerton shows how the decision scale[1] (see below) can allow users to make choices at different levels of importance and impact. Finding a good balance of decision choice is key to any successful game play or interaction design scenario.

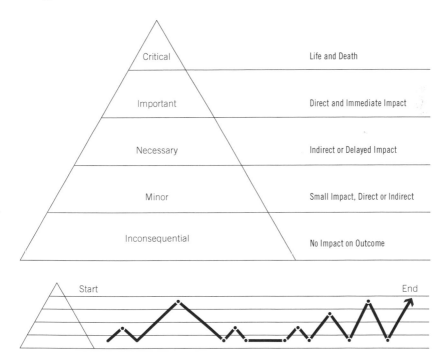

Critical	Life and Death
Important	Direct and Immediate Impact
Necessary	Indirect or Delayed Impact
Minor	Small Impact, Direct or Indirect
Inconsequential	No Impact on Outcome

As the game play progresses, there needs to be a good rhythm of important decisions to keep the user engaged yet enough less impactive ones to give the user time to rest.

If there is no balance, such as too many life and death or inconsequential decisions, the game play may be overwhelming or the user may get bored.

1 Game Design Workshop, A Playcentric Approach to Creating Innovative Games 2nd Edition by Tracy Fullerton

Denotation and Connotation

Denotation and connotation can both be used to describe imagery in written form, but have different contexts. Denotation is the direct meaning of an object; it is its pure definition without any emotions or associations to it. Connotation refers to the different ways people interpret an object, through emotions, beliefs or prior experiences.

Basketball

DENOTATION - Actual Meaning
"A usually indoor court game between two teams of usually five players each who score by tossing an inflated ball through a raised goal." [1]

CONNOTATION - Interpretation of Meaning
Child - Toy to play sports game with.
Mother - Child's toy to clean up.
Father - Game on TV.
Professional - Livelihood to earn money (see above).

Digital Tablet

DENOTATION - Actual Meaning
"A tablet PC is a wireless, portable personal computer with a touch screen interface " [2]

CONNOTATION - Interpretation of Meaning
Child - Toy to play digital games on (see above).
Mother - Distraction for kids.
Father - Expensive gift for him.
Professional - Tool for business.

1 http://www.merriam-webster.com/dictionary/basketball?show=0&t=1347671821
2 http://searchmobilecomputing.techtarget.com/definition/tablet-PC

Design Constraints

Design constraints are based on limitations of the boundary of the design system. Design components such as weight, dimensions, energy output, materials, cost and function all factor into the theory of design constraints. Design constraints can help form the scope of a project and set realistic design limitations. Design constraints shouldn't hamper creativity, but if you don't respect them, it may lead to design errors, added production time or higher project costs.

Ink Usage/Coverage

4 Color

3 Color

2 Color

1 Color

While GUI programs afford print designers the freedom of placement of type and graphics (left), the design constraints can be seen in the cost of the total amount of inks used to print the design. The more colors/amount used, the higher the cost it is to print the design (right).

Normal Document Flow

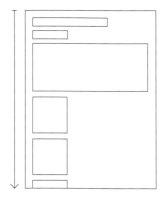

Web designers don't have the color constraints that print designers have. However Web browsers render information from top to bottom under the design constraint called "normal document flow" (left). Code must be used to float elements (right) to the left or right, which is why many Web pages work within a grid-like design system.

Design Patterns

Architect Christopher Alexander first discussed pattern language in his book *A Pattern Language*. Design patterns in interactive design go beyond style and are more than just visual repetition. They are similar/reusable solutions that have a working function often seen in interface and software design. Design patterns can appear in all stages of the design process, strategy/user experience, visual arrangement/design and functionality/behavior. There are many different types of design patterns; below are just two examples.

Blank Slate Page

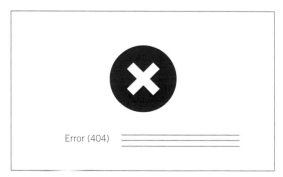

USER EXPERIENCE-BASED DESIGN PATTERN
When a user is signing up for a service or application, he is often presented with a page with no user information but an open slate for him to fill in. User experience designers need to tailor the page with interactions and sample information to encourage the user to fill in the information.

404 Error

BEHAVIOR-BASED DESIGN PATTERN
A 404 error page is a response from a server to a behavior by a browser when a user is searching for a page unable to access. Although there are many types of error pages, 404 deals with a Web page that is no longer there, has been moved or has changed.

Error (404)

Difference Threshold

Difference threshold also known as Weber's Law or Law of Just Noticeable Differences was named after psychologist Ernst Weber. Difference threshold happens when the minimum of change or difference is noticed in two different stimuli by a person. When applied to interactive design, knowing when there are noticeable changes may help the user better recognize hierarchy, notice key points of interest and help direct him through the overall experience.

Room Temperature Difference Threshold

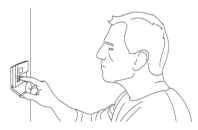

Two people are sitting in a living room and both feel cold. The current temperature in the room is 68°F degrees. One person raises it to 70°F degrees.

After the heat is turned up 2 degrees, only one of the two people feels a difference. The difference threshold for the other person may be 3 or 4 degrees higher.

Difference Threshold and Visual Hierarchy

← No Noticeable Difference

← Difference Threshold

← Clear Hierarchy

While there is a slight difference between the header (top rectangle) and subheader (bottom rectangle), it's too subtle to notice.

The difference threshold can be seen above, but the visual hierarchy is not strong.

Clear visual hierarchy helps create focus on title and stresses difference in the title elements.

Digital Skeuomorphs

In digital design, digital skeuomorphs give users the ability to make connections with objects that they are familiar with in the physical world. This connection allows designers to reinforce intended functions of their designs to the user. Digital skeuomorphs use visual translation and metaphor/metonymy as tools to communicate key visual points in digital design. They often show analog examples of digital theories and principles to help explain their meaning.

Visual Metonymy [1]

A paint bucket serves the function of holding paint for the user to dip a brush in and then paint a surface.

This digital tool icon of an abstract paint bucket serves as a visual metonymy to paint an area with a color on screen.

Digital Skeuomorph

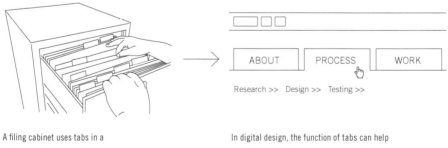

A filing cabinet uses tabs in a staggered format to label and separate each folder.

In digital design, the function of tabs can help separate different page options in a navigation system, similar to a filing cabinet.

---

1 Designing for the Digital Age: How to Create Human-Centered Products and Services by Kim Goodwin

Display Factors

Display devices are measured from one corner of the device to the opposite catty-corner. The screen is defined by the width x height, often viewed in units of pixels/points. A designer needs to take into consideration how different users will view their designs in various sizes/resolutions. It is important to understand that operating systems and Web browser components use compositional space from the overall design when targeting a device size.

Target Device Size

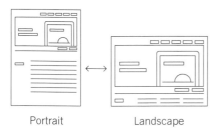

Higher screen resolution equates to more details which results in small icons, interface elements and more screen space (right). Lower screen resolution will result in the opposite: less space and larger screen elements (left).

Screen Components

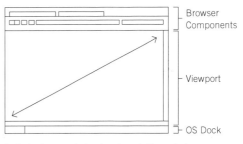

Designing for target device size only works if you take into consideration interface elements on the screen such as menu bars and browser components to attain the actual viewport area (arrows).

Liquid Layout

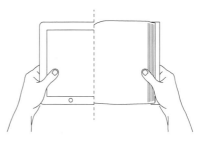

Portrait   Landscape

Designs may need to work in both a vertical (portrait) and horizontal (landscape) format, causing the content to fluidly change and hide when needed.

Ergonomic Factors

Printed books have margins for visual rest and placement of hands (right). Digital screens also need to address ergonomic factors, such as hand placement, that affect the user's experience (left).

Divergent and Convergent

Used for creative brainstorming sessions, divergent and convergent thinking allows for a full exploration of idea generation and conclusion. Divergent explores the idea of endless possibilities and the willingness to keep an open mind at all times. Convergent focuses on narrowing ideas and concepts down, clarifying goals and developing final conclusions. While powerful when used together, they are counterintuitive if they are used at the exact same time. The key is to know when to apply either one to a given situation; the results can yield a powerful result.

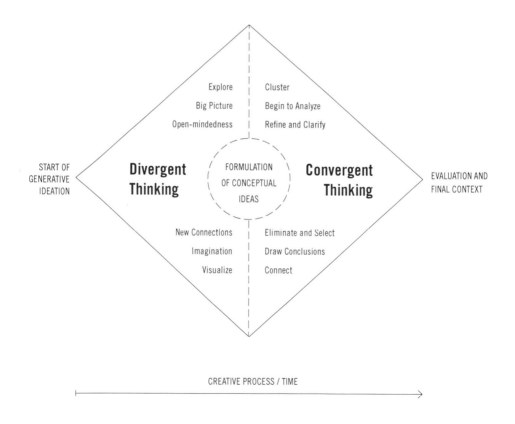

Entry Point

An effective entry point is important for first-time users because there may only be a few seconds to entice them to use a digital interface or enter a Web site. Entry point designs should have a clear hierarchy, and the decision choices should direct the user to a path within the content. A good analogy[1]: would a potential shopper be more enticed to enter a business storefront with an inviting, well-designed entry point or one with a lot of visual noise and confusion?

Physical / Storefront Entry Point

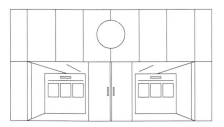

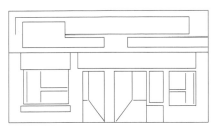

A clear entry point, has a balanced hierarchy and inviting visuals' support system. The branding is front and center with a strong product presence.

Overwhelming visual information, multiple points of entry, varying signals and no clear product preview might deter the shopper from entering.

Digital Interface Entry Point

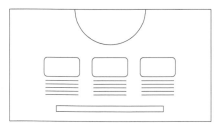

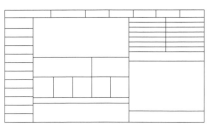

A well-designed entry point has a balanced hierarchy and clear decisions points for the user to select.

Too many decisions with no sense of hierarchy makes it difficult for the user to make a clear choice.

1 Entry Point / Storefront analogy: Designing Effective Entry Points in Web Design by Brandon Jones via tuts+

Eyetracking

Eyetracking is the technique and study of following a user's eye path while reading screen or print-based content. Using computer equipment and software to record activities allows researchers to better understand fixation points, which is when the eye rests on a particular area. The human eye connects fixation points together through rapid eye movements called saccades.

Eyetracking Equipment Scenario

Eyetracking equipment for digital studies varies. Software can record results into heat maps or gaze plots. A headset or computer screen camera can record user's behavior.

Heat Maps

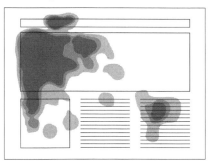

Heat maps show the user's fixation/saccades through heat-based gradation format. They can be used for a single experience or can merge multiple users' experiences into one study.

Gaze Plots

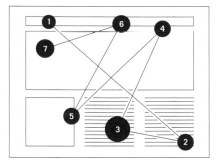

Gaze plots is when a single user is viewing a Web page and each fixation point is numbered and linked together in order. The longer the user stays on that point, the larger the circle becomes.

Facial Recognition

Studies[1] have shown that people have tendencies to look at a face more than any other image on a page. The user not only focuses on the face, but he also will look in the direction of where that face is looking, say to a product or tag line. This does not mean the user will maintain focus in that directed area, just that it will be directed there.

Face Recognition

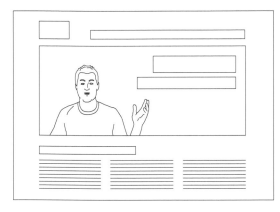

The face in the feature content section may help capture the viewer's attention to that area faster than another type of image or text.

Face Recognition and Look Direction

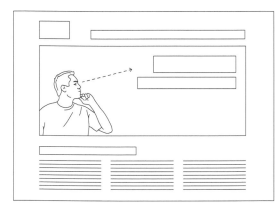

Once the viewer focuses on the face, his eyes may follow what direction it's looking. This may lead to a key phrase or important button choice.

1 http://usableworld.com.au/2009/03/16/you-look-where-they-look/

Faux Choice

Faux choice (or false choice) is when a decision between multiple choices ends in the same outcome. This term misleads the user into thinking that he has a true decision to make, but does not. Faux choice helps in controlling overgrown system outcomes and keeps the path of the user in the direction the designer wants. It should not be confused with wrong choice, which is when the user loses out on the decision.

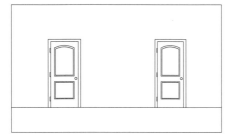

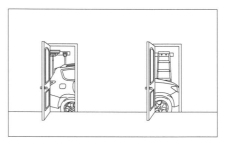

In this decision there are two doors within a house to choose from. One may go outside and the other may go to the garage.

This is a faux choice, because both doors go to the garage. The poor design may lead to confusion to people unfamiliar with the house.

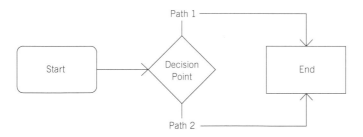

In the digital realm, a game or digital experience can use faux choice to guide the user to the same outcome no matter the path/choice. When used correctly, it can direct the user to the intended outcome, but if overused it could cause confusion similar to the door example above.

Feedback

When a user has indicated an action or completed a task, the system or product will respond to the user to reinforce that action has happened. Feedback can be communicated in various reaction times (sometimes milliseconds) and different forms, such as an auditory sound, physical action, verbal response, visual cue or a combination. Feedback can help in relaying if a choice was positive or negative in the user's experience.

Visual and Auditory Feedback

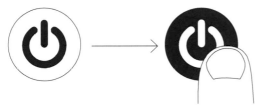

In this example, a user presses a universal power button and receives feedback visually through light and auditory by a "bing" or "bong" sound depending on the device.

Data/Information Process Feedback

A popup dialogue box is a type of visual feedback that tells the user that there needs to be more information inputted into a field or redirect the course of action.

Fitts's Law

Fitts's law is a formula that defines the time it takes for a person to move a mouse from one point on the screen to another point on the screen. This human-driven task involves the cursor at rest and a target located in a different position. In some cases to increase human computer interaction performance, target areas (navigation or button links) should be positioned in an area near a neutral cursor position. One could make Fitts's law work better if the button/nav items were closer together or larger in size, but this needs to be balanced with aesthetic considerations.

Fitts's Law Visualized

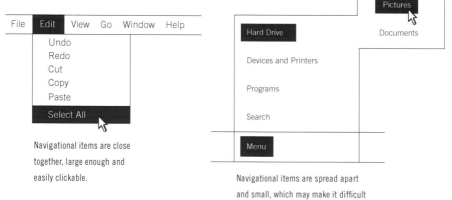

Efficient Use

Navigational items are close together, large enough and easily clickable.

Inefficient Use

Navigational items are spread apart and small, which may make it difficult to select.

Flowchart

Flowcharts represent a sequence of steps of a given operation, action or process. They use a series of graphics that include geometric shapes, arrows and reference keys to describe their function. Flowcharts may allow groups to build a common understanding, improve upon current processes and create a greater consistency in their workflow. Flowcharts show a basic view of information flow, where a data flow or usability diagram shows a higher level of system flow/complexity.

Online Banking Flowchart

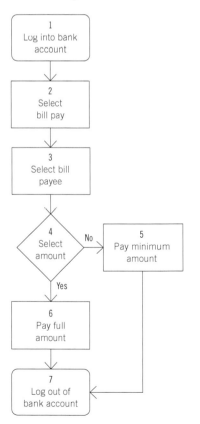

Flowchart Symbol Key [1]

The start and end of a task has rounded corners to help separate it from an action.

Rectangles most often are used to describe an action or page in a sequence-based process.

Decisions have more than one path and a yes or no tells which direction is preferred.

Control flow arrows show what direction or step to follow to next.

* Rectangles can be interpreted as an action/ task or page [2] depending on if context is based on user choices, document flow or a combination of the two.

1 Flowcharts: Plain & Simple: Learning & Application Guide by Joiner Associates Staff, p. 12
2 Jesse James Garrett's – A visual vocabulary for describing information architecture and interaction design

Flow State

Dr. Mihaly Csikszentmihalyi's studies and writings on the state of flow have pioneered the term in modern society today. Flow state[1] happens when a person is highly engaged / immersed in an experience or task and loses sense of time and is less aware of what is happening around him. Experiences can range from a game, writing, creative performance to standard work activity. Different cultures and people may achieve flow in different ways.

Flow State Diagram [2]

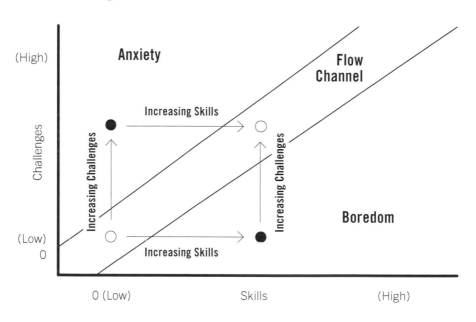

The flow channel is the area between challenge and skills that balances anxiety and boredom for a user during an experience or task.

1 Csikszentmihalyi, Mihaly. (1990). Flow – the Psychology of Optimal Experience. New York: Harper Perennial.
2 Diagram: Anxiety, Boredom and Flow (Csikszentmihalyi, 1990) (captions added van Gorp, 2006)

Musical Flow State

When playing the guitar, a person can fall into a state of flow. If he is in control and feeling what is happening, the sense of time may be lost.

If the person forgets the lyrics or gets distracted from an outside source, the flow state may stop.

Gaming Flow State

Games that balance achievable goals and interesting narratives can help the user get into the flow state.

Breaking a game into stages allows the user intermittent rest while staying within the flow state.

An incoming phone call may interrupt the game play and stop the state of flow.

Fogg Behavior Model

Scientist BJ Fogg developed the Fogg Behavior Model[1] to address what causes behavior change. To achieve a behavior trigger, the core motivators (such as acceptance, hope, rejection, fear, etc.) need to line up with ability factors (such as time, money, physical effort, etc.). Triggers can be anything from a cell phone ring to picking up and eating a cookie by simply walking past a cookie jar. Action-based triggers found in digital interaction design are call-to-action buttons, clickable links or information entry that can be acted upon now.

Fogg Behavior Model

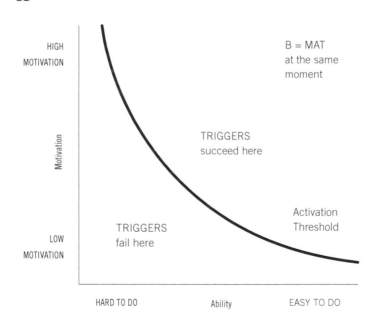

1 www.behaviormodel.org

Low Ability and Motivation

An example of a trigger that may fail is when someone is driving by a billboard advertisement and cannot act (low ability) upon it and is not interested (low motivation) in purchasing that product at that moment in time.

High Ability and Motivation

 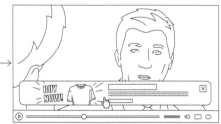

An example of a "signal" trigger is when someone is watching a video online and an ad pops up for him to purchase a product linked to the ad.

At that moment in time the user needs (motivated) the product and can (ability) click on that link to make the purchase, thus acting upon the trigger instantaneously.

Frame Mobility

Frame mobility[1] is the concept of dividing a larger scene or object into separate divisions while continuously keeping part of the subject within the viewing frame. By breaking down the larger context, it allows one to show a process, build a narrative or create a preview onto what will happen later. To help stage the content, text may accompany the scene when it pauses or stops for visual rest.

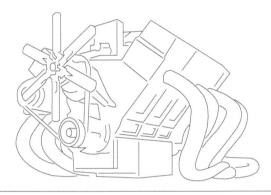

1

2
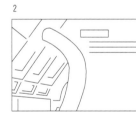

3
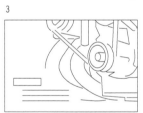

4
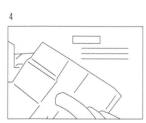

5

6
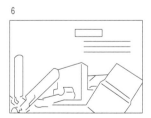

The above example shows a car motor as a whole. The following panels show it in a motion sequence broken down into separate scenes, with titles and written descriptions.

1 Motion Graphic Design: Applied History and Aesthetics by Jon S. Krasner

Gamification

Gamification[1] is the concept of applying gaming principles and theory to non-gaming applications. By adding game mechanics to non-gaming scenarios, such as learning applications, employment training sessions or social media campaigns, an experience can go from being a chore to a sense of play. Gamification helps to create an immersive brand experience to keep users more engaged and willing to share products and services with others.

Gamification Scenario

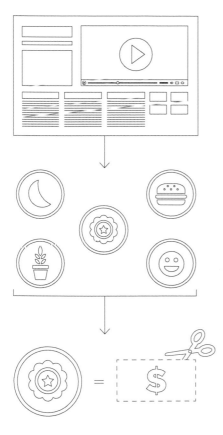

Participants engage in online branded activities such as watching videos, exploring pages on a site or sharing information with others.

Each activity earns participants the ability to unlock achievements to earn badges or points.

Badges may allow participants to enter contests, get discounts on products or attain brand-based freebies.

1 http://gamification.org/

Geon Theory

Geon theory or recognition-by-components theory was developed by Dr. Irving Biederman. The theory states that we recognize and break down objects we see into a basic group of shapes. By using recognizable building blocks or shapes (geons), the viewer will start to think about what the object is, rather than what it looks like. The geon theory states that when objects are broken down into their elementary shapes, they are easier to render.

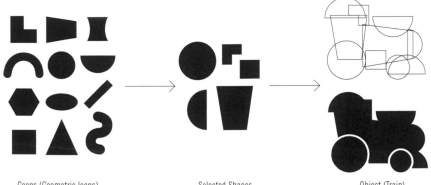

Geons (Geometric Icons)   Selected Shapes   Object (Train)

Examples in Visual Design

ICON

Icons are abstract symbols that represent a function or process. They are often seen in interface design. *Ex. Download Arrow Icon*

PICTOGRAM

Pictograms are pictorial representation images that are used in place of words or phrases to communicate their meaning. *Ex. Cycling 1968 Summer Olympics*

ISOTYPE

Isotype (International System of Typographic Picture Education) is a well-known pictogram system used in Europe in the 1940s to 1960s. *Ex. Isotype by Gerd Arntz*

Grid Systems

A grid is an underlining structure that supports a design based on alignments, object relationships and grid-based components. Grid systems can vary in numbers of columns and can be simple or complex. If used correctly, a grid will enhance the content to make the information reflect the designer's intention and goals. While grids add structure to a design, they should be balanced with the rhythmic intent of the content.

Column Grid	**Modular Grid**	**Hierarchical Grid**

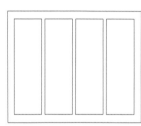 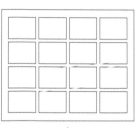 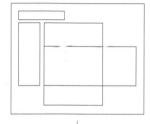

 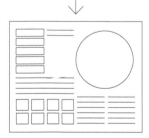 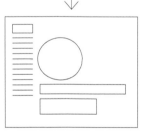

Column grid systems have vertical alignments that work well for running text, block areas and are flexible for varying content.

Modular grid systems are used for involved content. They use horizontal thresholds to create subdivisions labeled modules. Modules work together to create spatial zones of interaction to further support content.

For content that does not fit into a column or modular grid, a hierarchical grid system may be used. Alignments and organizations are based on the unique elements in the content and can vary greatly within the design.

Hick's Law

Hick's law was named after psychologist William Hick and states that the more choices one has, the more time it will take to process a decision. While some people might want more options, their reaction time will be slowed and sometimes even stopped due to all the different choices. There are many factors that go into the effects of Hick's law such as a person's experience, the type of choices, the category of choices and the way they are presented.

Grocery Store Jams Sampling [1]

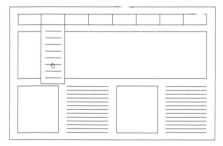

A study found that customers are less likely to try a smaller sampling, but those who do try are more likely to purchase jams if the sampling choices are limited to 6.

If there are 24 to 30 choices of jams, there is a higher chance of someone sampling them, but a lower chance of a jam being purchased. This illustrates that more choices is not always better, if the end goal is to have someone purchase the jam.

Digital Interface Menu

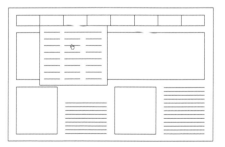

Users may be more willing to use a drop-down menu that is a single list and with limited choices.

A larger fly-out menu with multiple columns and subdivisions may be overwhelming, more difficult to make a correct choice, and in some cases may cause the user to opt out from searching.

1 Iyengar, Shena S. and Mark R. Lepper 2000. When choice is demotivating: Can one desire too much of a good thing? Journal of Personality and Social Psychology. 79:995-1006)

Hot and Cool Media

Hot and cool media[1] measures the levels of participation a person invests in engaging in media. The media is considered hot if it has a high level of definition or resolution, causing the audience to use less effort to be engaged. The media is considered cool if its definition is low, forcing the participant to be more involved. If there is less active detail, the audience must work more to fill in the missing information.

Hot Media

Someone watching a movie can be totally immersed into the media without significant effort. This example emphasizes the sense of vision, hence describing it as hot media.

Cool Media

When reading a printed comic book, the user is required to be more active in viewing this type of media. It is viewed as cool media since the user has to work at viewing multiple panels and pages to get the full narrative experience.

1 Understanding Media: The Extensions of Man by Marshall McLuhan

Hub and Spoke Paradigm

Used in distribution, computer network systems and directional structures, hub and spoke is an analogy of a wheel where each path is connected off a central area. The main hub is where the person, products or information is distributed from. To travel down a different path, they must return to the central hub first. The benefits of this model include clear context, ease of use and easily expandable.

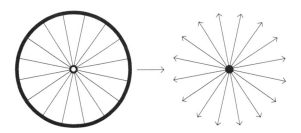

Imagine if the outer rim was taken away from a bike wheel, but the hub and all the spokes were still there (left). The only way to get to the outer edges from another edge is through the middle hub.

Physical Hub Distribution

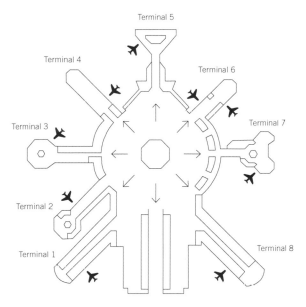

Terminal 5

Terminal 4

Terminal 6

Terminal 3

Terminal 7

Terminal 2

Terminal 1

Terminal 8

In airport travel, hub and spoke can be seen in the layout of an airport. The center hub is where passengers check flight times, use facilities and wait for a plane to arrive. Each terminal represents a spoke to reach their intended flight.

Interface Design Hub and Spoke [1]

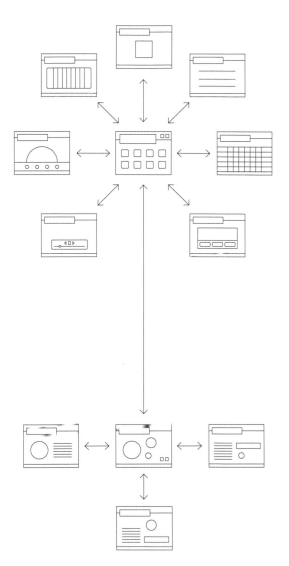

In a gaming app, the hub is the central navigation (landing screen) in which subdirectories of an application can be accessed. This system of back and forth helps control user flow and reduce misdirection.

EXPENDABILITY / SUBDIRECTORY
In some cases the main pages will become hubs and connect to subpages through its spokes. Unless there is a master navigation, the user will have to go back two steps to get back to the home screen.

1 Designing Interfaces: Patterns for Effective Interaction Design by Jenifer Tidwell

Infinite Canvas

Comicbook theorist Scott McCloud invented the Infinite Canvas[1] to push the concept that screen content truly never ends. The idea of content being presented on one page is an option for the designer/creator. This window presentation allows a variety of interaction scenarios, information organizations and narrative structures. Instead of a hard page dimension, the only concerns with an infinite content plane is screen size and resolution.

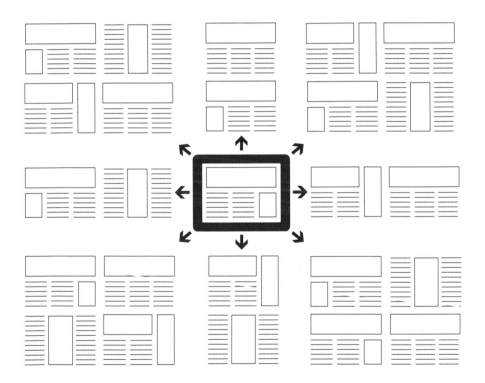

1 Reinventing Comics: How Imagination and Technology Are Revolutionizing an Art Form by Scott McCloud

Machine Learning

Machine learning is based on the idea of computer programs taking data, analyzing it to create meaningful interpretations and making future decisions based on that. Most often the data is processed by an algorithm (which is a step-by-step breakdown of a computer process). Application types such as predictions, clustering and recommendations can come out of machine learning.

Advanced Parking Guidance System

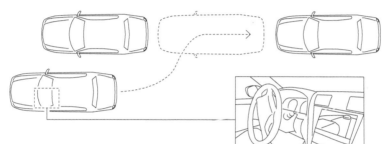

This physical example is a combination of computer vision, heuristics and machine learning. The car learns to self-park itself based on the visual data presented to it.

Spam Filtering System

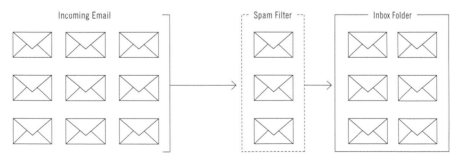

Algorithms are created from information such as recurring patterns, subject line characteristics and sender information. Using that knowledge, email programs can create filters to differentiate between spam (junk mail) and real email.

Maslow's Hierarchy of Needs

Understanding what the user is thinking is very important in interaction design, but often overlooked is the basic needs of human beings. Psychologist Abraham Maslow developed the concept of hierarchy of needs that suggests that people need to fulfill their basic needs before moving to more complex psychological and social needs. Maslow's hierarchy of needs is often shown in a pyramid diagram, with the basic needs at the bottom and the more complex psychological needs at the top.

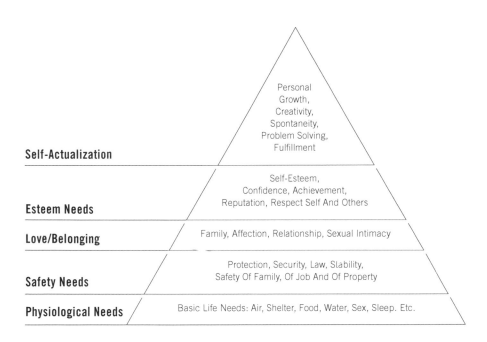

Self-Actualization

Personal Growth, Creativity, Spontaneity, Problem Solving, Fulfillment

Esteem Needs

Self-Esteem, Confidence, Achievement, Reputation, Respect Self And Others

Love/Belonging

Family, Affection, Relationship, Sexual Intimacy

Safety Needs

Protection, Security, Law, Stability, Safety Of Family, Of Job And Of Property

Physiological Needs

Basic Life Needs: Air, Shelter, Food, Water, Sex, Sleep. Etc.

Mediated Reality

Mediated reality[1] is when a digital device or display adjusts or augments what the user is seeing. In general it is a framework for adding virtual content to modify a human's perception. There are subsets of mediated reality such as augmented, virtual and modulated reality, as seen in the diagram below.

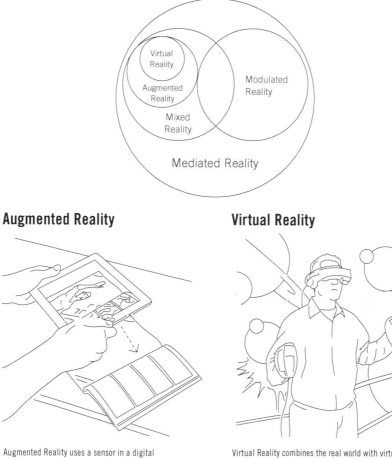

Augmented Reality

Virtual Reality

Augmented Reality uses a sensor in a digital display to augment a user's perception with virtual information not in the real environment.

Virtual Reality combines the real world with virtual elements in the same time and space to create a simulated environment.

1 Mediated Reality with implementations for everyday life, Presence Connect, MIT Press journal, by Steve Mann

Mental Model

The definition of a mental model varies greatly depending on the point of view or resource. In general it's a strategy to help UX designers understand the user's prior experiences, assumptions and skills levels using a product, digital device or interface. Mental models can also be represented in an alignment diagram (see right) of the user's relationships to the environment, behaviors and previous actions in part of creating a strategic approach to understanding one's thought process.

Mental Model User's Process

When a user is engaged in a new task, he forms decisions based on previous experiences to create a self-working knowledge base or mental model. If the design is similar to prior experiences, he has a greater chance of success. The process above shows one user's mental model thought process.

1 Visual/Auditory/Kinesthetic Analysis
2 Mental Formulation of Previous Experiences
3 Creation of Mental Model
4 User Tests Mental Model / Heuristics
5 Completion of Task or Redo Process

Affinity/Alignment Diagram of Mental Model [1]

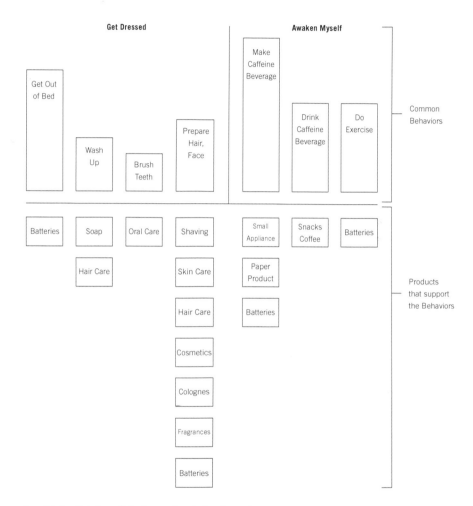

Once data is collected, an affinity diagram allows for the alignment
of common behaviors (on top) to compare with supporting product
features (on bottom) to gain a better understanding of user's interests.

1 Mental Models: Aligning Design Strategy with Human Behavior by Indi Young

Minimum Usable Design

Influenced from the concept of MVP (minimum viable product), where only the minimum features are released for initial sale, minimum usable design focuses on the Web design process instead of a physical product. Paul Scrivens coined the term minimum usable design[1] to talk to the idea of when a design is usable for a large part (say 50%) of the intended audience without actually being complete. While some would say a design is truly never done, at the very least if the progress can be properly evaluated, the rest of the project can be prioritized to not waste resources or time. Also see Pareto Principle.

Web Design Process

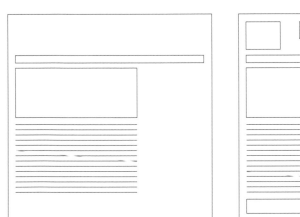

The initial design has a navigation and main content. It meets 50% of the design needed for the intended user.

Further in the process, other features such as social media, advertisement space and other secondary content may be added, but each part may take up as much time as the initial design did even though it is not as proportionally important.

---

1 http://www.smashingmagazine.com/2012/05/29/mud-minimum-usable-design by Paul Scrivens

Multi-Touch Gestures

Multi-touch gestures are various operations and movements between a user's hand, touch pad or multi-touch device. The gestures may vary between devices and operating systems. Below are some common gestures and their functions.

TAP
Tapping once or twice allows the user to click or double-click a selection.

PRESS / HOLD
By pressing down and holding, the user can create a longer selection and secondary options.

SCROLL (Two Fingers)
Two fingers next to each other sliding up and down will move the page in that direction.

PINCH (Zoom in / out)
By moving a finger and thumb in and out in a pinch-like motion, you can zoom in and out of a photo or page.

FLICK or SWIPE
These techniques of quickly moving the fingers right and left may navigate the user to pages or objects in a defined book or page section.

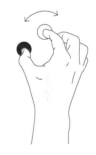

ROTATE
By using the thumb and fingers in a clockwise motion (or counterclockwise) the user can turn objects in that rotational direction.

Page Fold

In Web design there is an imaginary line that creates a fold or separation of content on the page before scrolling is started. The content that is seen by the viewer is known as "above the fold" and tends to have more importance, whereas content below the fold is given secondary awareness. The term above the fold comes from editorial design where a newspaper's fold generally cuts the front page content in half, forcing the designer to consider what to put on the top half.

Newspaper Page Fold [1]   Digital Design Page Fold

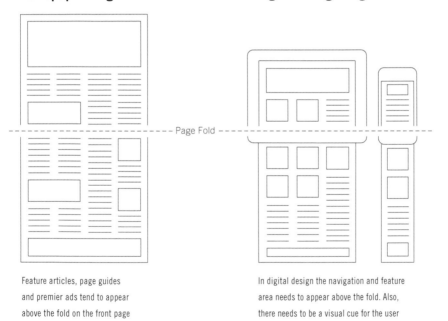

Feature articles, page guides and premier ads tend to appear above the fold on the front page of a newspaper.

In digital design the navigation and feature area needs to appear above the fold. Also, there needs to be a visual cue for the user to scroll to see the content below the fold.

1 Above the Fold: Understanding the Principles of Successful Web Site Design by Brian Miller

The Pareto Principle

Also known as the "80-20 Rule" the Pareto Principle is when approximately 80% of the results are created from 20% of the actions. The term was named after Vilfredo Pareto, an Italian economist who stated that 80% of Italians' land was owned by 20% of the population in the early 1900s. In an interactive project, if most of it (80%) is completed in the strategy/user experience stage (20%) of the project process, then the majority of focus and emphasis should be applied there.

Italy Land Ownership

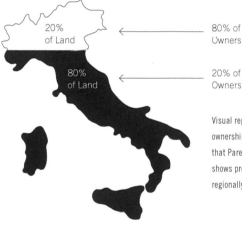

20%
of Land

80%
of Land

80% of the
Ownership Population

20% of the
Ownership Population

Visual representation of land
ownership in Italy in the 1960s
that Pareto stated. Note: Graph
shows proportion only and is not
regionally specific.

Interactive Project Process

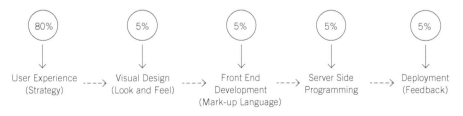

80%	5%	5%	5%	5%
User Experience (Strategy)	Visual Design (Look and Feel)	Front End Development (Mark-up Language)	Server Side Programming	Deployment (Feedback)

Certain projects may have the majority of the work done (top
row) in one section, which is 20% of the overall process
(bottom row). Note: This may be an extreme example.

Personas

Personas are a type of user model that allow designers to predict how users will act and think, and why they want to accomplish a given task. Personas are a composite archetype and not based on a real person, but a combination of motivations and behaviors. They are not made up and, if done right, are based on factual data recorded beforehand in the observation research stage. In the end the persona will address a specific type of person (not one specific person) and not a random group of users.

"I get very frustrated when I cannot find what I am looking for."

Frank

Demographics
Age: 55
Occupation: Teacher
Location: White Plains, NY

Goals
Wants to find discounts online.
Doesn't want to spend a lot of time on one page.
Prefers newer products over old products.

User Behaviors
Scans through reviews of products quickly.
Likes to share deals (information) with others.
Gets distracted easily.

Personas can help designers to determine, communicate and measure a product's goals or usage. While personas vary in range of content, they tend to always have a person's name, photo, quote and basic demographic information.

Poka-Yoke Principle

Coined by industrial engineer Shigeo Shingo, Poka-Yoke means fail-safing in Japanese. Poka-Yoke is when a physical constraint is applied to an object or task so it will become error proof. In most cases the shape and space should be enough to signal to the users if the interaction will or will not work, but even if they try, the physical dimensions will stop them from the wrong execution.

Physical Poka-Yoke

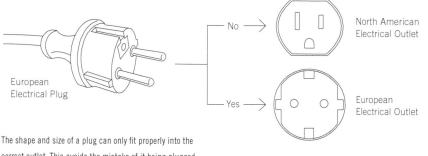

European
Electrical Plug

No →

North American
Electrical Outlet

Yes →

European
Electrical Outlet

The shape and size of a plug can only fit properly into the
correct outlet, This avoids the mistake of it being plugged
into the wrong slot.

CAPTCHA

While there is not a clear-cut and dry digital Poka-Yoke example, somewhat
close might be the use of a CAPTCHA[1]. A common type of CAPTCHA[2] is word-
recognition, which is often seen in a sign-up process. By having to visually
translate content, the sign-up program will know if it's a real person and not an
automated spamming program.

1 CAPTCHA: Completely Automated Public Turing test to tell Computers and Humans Apart
2 Coined in 2000 by Luis von Ahn, Manuel Blum, Nicholas Hopper and John Langford of Carnegie Mellon University

Principle of Least Effort

Harvard University linguistics professor George Zipf coined the term principle of least effort and then was connected to information research/seeking by librarian Thomas Mann. The theory is that humans by nature create patterns of useful behaviors that allow ease (path of least resistance). When followed, these patterns can result in the least possible effort. In many cases the least amount of effort may yield a lesser result.

Classroom Lab Setting

A student might ask her neighboring student a question because it requires the least amount of effort. This choice may not fully answer the question and take more time to figure out.

But if the student would raise her hand, wait for the instructor to come over and answer the question, it might yield a better result and save time, even though it would require more effort.

Search Box as Spell Check

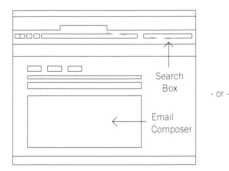

Search Box

Email Composer

- or -

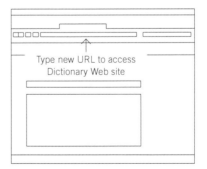

Type new URL to access Dictionary Web site

When composing an email, if the users cannot correctly spell a word, they may use the search box to get the correct spelling instead of accessing a dictionary program/site.

While using the search box may give the desired result, it doesn't always break the word down phonetically or give a definition that will help the user learn it for the long term.

Qualitative vs. Quantitative

While they both deal with data, they are different in how they are used. Qualitative data represents the quality and helps describe the meaning (words) and appearance (images). Qualitative research helps define the problem and the understanding of different groups' opinions and decisions, whereas quantitative data deals with measuring by numeral statistics and quantity analysis. Quantitative research deals with the final conclusion and helps identify larger segments' choices.

Qualitative Data **Quantitative Data**

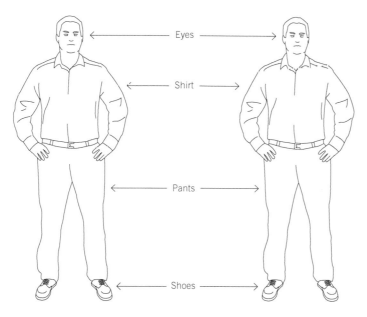

Eyes: Blue
Shirt: Casual Collar Dress
Pants: Tan Khaki Pants
Shoes: Leather Soles Shoes

Eyes: R:144 G:181 B:210
Shirt: 17 Neck / 34-35 Sleeve Length
Pants: 36 Waist / 34 Length
Shoes: Size 12

Reading Distances

Digital Book expert Craig Mod breaks tablet reading distances into three main categories: Bed, Knee and Breakfast[1]. Bed refers to a close-to-face distance where the reader is lying in bed with the digital tablet. Knee refers to a medium distance where the user is reading the digital tablet while sitting on/in a chair and the tablet on the lap/knee. Breakfast refers to the far-from-face distance, as if the user was reading the tablet on the table while eating breakfast without holding the tablet. Ideally the content can be adjusted per reading distance to create the optimal viewing experience.

Bed (Close to Face)

Knee (Medium Distance)

Breakfast (Far from Face)

1 Bed, Knee and Breakfast by Craig Mod

Responsive Design

Responsive design[1], sometimes called Adaptive design, is the technique and idea where content responds to the platform it is being viewed on based on the device properties. It's based on the idea of flexibility, whereby by the structure, imagery or media truly adapts, by either repositioning, changing size, adjusting view state or eliminating content based on the user's needs. While the examples below show a desktop monitor, tablet and mobile device, the concept can be applied to other media such as TV entertainment systems, vehicle interfaces or any type of Web-accessible digital device.

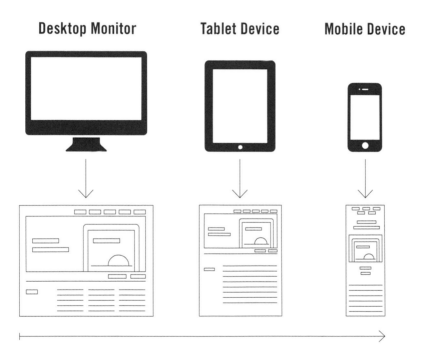

Desktop Monitor

Tablet Device

Mobile Device

Full desktop monitor view, with a four-column grid system, imagery and navigation at 100%.

At tablet view, the imagery and navigation are decreased in size. The grid system is collapsed and the text forms into one large paragraph.

At mobile device view, the navigation becomes stacked, imagery is further receded, and copy fits into one column.

1 Responsive Web Design by Ethan Marcotte

Rules of Play

Before developing an operational scheme of a game, an understanding of the rules must be established. In the book *Rules of Play*, authors Katie Salen and Eric Zimmerman break down the rules into three categories[1]. Operational rules are the written-out rules that come with the game. Constitutive rules are the logical and mathematical rules of the game. Implicit rules are the unwritten rules that are connected to etiquette and sportsmanship. The rules of play can be applied to board games, video games and online games. Below is an example of tic-tac-toe and how the rules of play apply to it.

Operational Rules

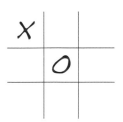

Rules of Play: Players use a board that has three rows and three columns. Players take time alternating between placing X's and O's.

Constitutive Rules

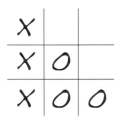

The rules based on math: for example a player needs to get three of the same characters in a row to win.

Implicit Rules

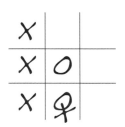

Players should not cheat: for example they will not skip the other player's turn or take a position already chosen.

---

1 Rules of Play: Game Design Fundamentals by Katie Salen and Eric Zimmerman

Scanning vs. Reading

While specific situations (goals, time or user experience) differ greatly, studies[1] have shown that users tend not to intently read a Web page as they would a printed book; they merely scan the page. In his book *Don't Make Me Think: A Common Sense Approach to Web Usability* Steve Krug discusses how users make sacrifices and choose the most reasonable option[2]. Sacrifices are made because if the option they choose does not work, they can go back a page and try again with no real negative consequences. Clear hierarchy is key to establish levels of importance and reading direction.

Gutenberg Z

A typical long form print reading experience (in Western languages) might look like the above. Gutenberg Z pattern works left to right and top to bottom. This experience is void of interactive functions and major distractions.

Digital Scanning Experience

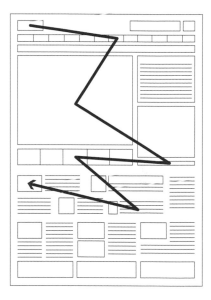

In most cases the user will scan the Web site or digital interface until something closely meets what he is looking for and choose that.

1 http://www.poynter.org/extra/eyetrack2004/viewing.htm
2 Don't Make Me Think: A Common Sense Approach to Web Usability, by Steve Krug

Sequence and Motion

To understand sequence and motion, going beyond a definition is essential. There must be an understanding of their relationship and the differences between the two. The discipline of film and animation (the process of making a motion picture) needs to be analyzed. Through persistence of vision, sequence becomes motion.

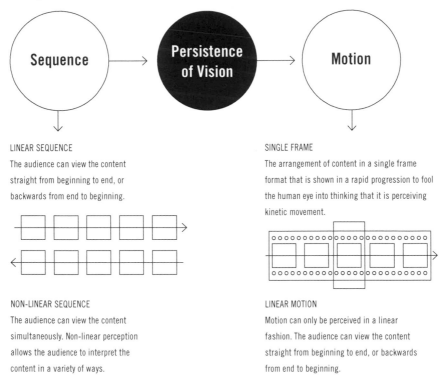

LINEAR SEQUENCE

The audience can view the content straight from beginning to end, or backwards from end to beginning.

SINGLE FRAME

The arrangement of content in a single frame format that is shown in a rapid progression to fool the human eye into thinking that it is perceiving kinetic movement.

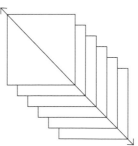

NON-LINEAR SEQUENCE

The audience can view the content simultaneously. Non-linear perception allows the audience to interpret the content in a variety of ways.

LINEAR MOTION

Motion can only be perceived in a linear fashion. The audience can view the content straight from beginning to end, or backwards from end to beginning.

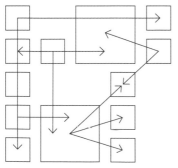

Sequence Mapping

In her book *Designing Interfaces*[1], Jenifer Tidwell used the term sequence mapping as a way to label multi-step selection processes. Sequence mapping serves as two functions, showing where a user is at in a step-by-step experience and how much progress still needs to be done. In most cases sequence mapping is a linear process that has a concise description of what each step is, number in process and allowing for back and forth selection between multiple steps.

Steps Left

This multi-step process shows what steps were taken (in black) and where the user is (dotted highlight) at in the overall progress. This type of sequencing is seen in application or sign-up processes. It is most often seen at the top of a page's design.

Pagination

Web sites that have multiple pages such as articles, online forum or long-form page documentation are often created dynamic text but can vary in style. This form of sequence mapping is seen at the bottom of the page.

---

1 *Designing Interfaces: Patterns for Effective Interaction Design* by Jenifer Tidwell

Shannon and Weaver Communication Model

Mathematicians Claude Shannon and Warren Weaver originally designed the communication model for electrical signal transmission. The model demonstrates how any form of communication can be misunderstood due to the many stages of transmission. While this model is linear, it is the basis for a number of other non-linear theories of source (sender) to destination (receiver) communication.

Shannon and Weaver Model

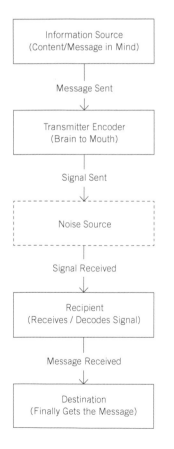

Non-Linar Interactive Model

Digital messaging is an example of non-linear communication. A message is in the sender's mind; he must type out (encode) the words on the digital interface and then send. The receiver opens the message, reads it (decodes), processes its meaning. The original sender awaits for feedback and becomes the new receiver from the person the message was sent to.

Signals and Cues

Signals are visual or audible indications that interaction is taking place to activate or change a particular object. The cue is the response that the signal has been activated. In the physical world we see signals and cues everywhere, such as handles on a toaster oven or buttons on a gaming controller. Digital devices demonstrate signals and cues through icons/graphics, visual metaphors and transmission of sounds. Also see Affordances and Button States.

Gaming Controllers

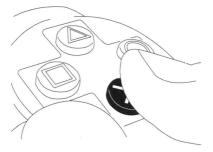

This physical signal is very clear because the button is raised and represents something to press. The cue is reinforced when it gets pressed down and an audible sound from the game is made.

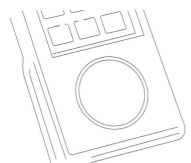

This signal in this controller is poorly designed because the interaction area is flat with no visual directions. The user may not know where to click, press or turn.

Digital Interface

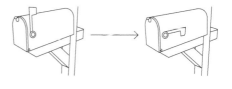

ADDITION

A mailbox signals mail pickup when the flag is raised (top). In digital messaging, the user knows email is in the inbox when there is an addition of a symbol or number (bottom). The cue follows when the flag is put down or symbol goes away.

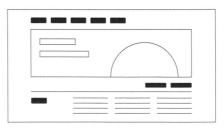

CONSISTENCY

Consistent styling (i.e. color) for navigation, buttons and links may allow users to recognize signals at a faster rate. Whatever the cue change is, it should also be consistent.

Site Map

Site maps are diagrams that show the flow information and structure of how pages on a Web site are grouped and organized. They allow the stakeholders to see the high-level view of a site, whereas wireframes allow for a page view. While site maps appear simple in design, one should always maintain proper alignment, text placement and a correct labeling/number system. If a site map becomes more complex, notations or a legend might be necessary.

Basic Site Map Example

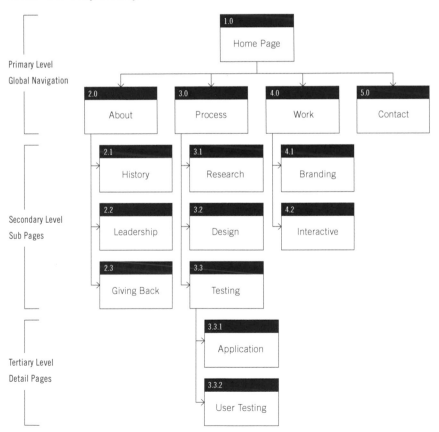

While a site map may look like a simple arrangement of boxes and lines, it's the subtle details that can make the page-to-page communication clear or confusing. Below are some examples of common mistakes made when creating a site map.

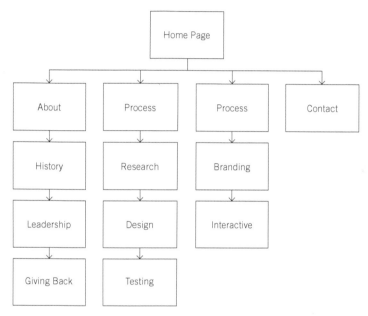

One continuous line through multiple pages communicates a forced linear option for the user. There is no way to navigate across all the pages in one click.

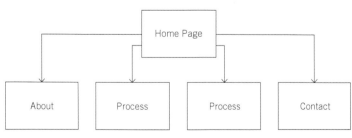

The above example shows the lack of global navigation. The user must go back to the home page before being able to select other sections.

Tesler's Law of the Conservation of Complexity

Larry Tesler, one of the interaction design forefathers, created the theory "Tesler's Law of the Conservation of Complexity." Tesler's law is the theory that each interaction process/system has a certain level of complexity. Designs can only be simplified up to a certain point; beyond that point the complexity can only be shifted. If the system needs to be simplified for the user, then it may become more difficult for the designer/developer to create/manage or vice versa. The transfer of complexity can either be on the surface (visual) or hidden (underlying functionality).

Soda Machine - Dispensing Soda Can and Change [1]

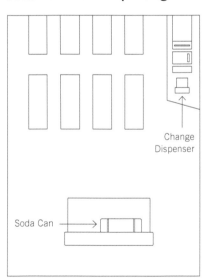

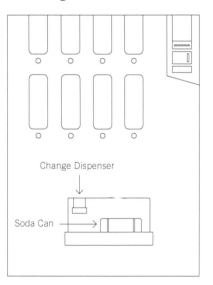

One type of soda vending machine might have the soda can come out of the bottom and the change in a separate area to the right below the money insert. This forces the users to go to two different places in this soda-buying experience.

Another type of soda vending machine might have the soda can and change come out in the same area. While this makes it easier for the user, the complexity shifts to the machine designer/maker.

1 *Creating a Good User Experience by Brian Miller via How Interactive Design*

While digital interfaces and computer scenarios might seem more complex than the soda machine experience example, the main idea is the same. The complexity limit does not change; it is shifted from one side to the other. The examples below are of a video chat call; in both you need a person's ID to make the call.

Video Chat Call

Hand Typing ID

Automated History List

The first time the user calls, he needs to type in the person's ID, then press call. This is a relatively simple interaction experience.

The second time the user attempts to call, the program may remember the user's ID in the recent history or after a character or two is typed. While easier for the user to select, the program needs to handle the complexity of remembering recent ID's.

Touch Target

Touch target refers to the target area of a digital button or link in relation to a person's finger size. The term has most concern with mobile interface design, whereas screen size needs to be balanced with content layout. The various developers of mobile devices have varying guidelines for touch target sizes.

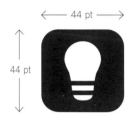

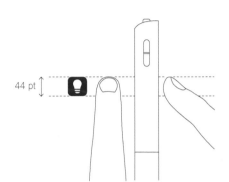

Sizes of touch targets can be measured in pixels (resolutions based) or in points and may change across devices. 44 by 44 is one type of minimum size guideline that may be used.

In this example the button matches the average finger size (top view). When the finger interacts with the digital screen (side view) it is often tilted to attain the optimal touch target.

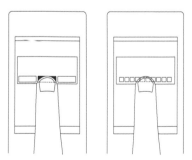

The button needs the proper touch target size and recognition area to reinforce the correct choice of the button (left). Improper proximity of buttons around the touch target may cause incorrect selections (right).

Some mobile games require the use of both thumbs to navigate the interface. This requires the designer to take into consideration that thumbs touch the target size, which is larger than the index finger.

Ubiquitous Computing

Before the Internet, social networking, universal file types or even GUI operating systems, computers were seen as stationary appliances. Mark Weiser coined the term ubiquitous computing, which is the integration of technology and human computer interaction within our everyday lives. The term covers all aspects of human interactions from finding and exchanging information, directional signals, and virtual information display in our everyday environment.

Ubiquitous Computing Scenario

1 CLOUD COMPUTING
While out, you access your shopping list on your home computer via the cloud (Internet) on a mobile device.

2 AUGMENTED REALITY
Through augmented reality, a print ad gives you directions to a store within walking distance where you can purchase the product on your list.

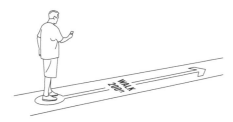

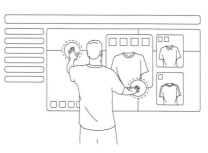

3 VIRTUAL WAYFINDING
On the way to the store, electronic directional cues signal a path on the walkway to guide you to your destination.

4 MULTI-GESTURE INTERFACES
At the store a digital screen allows the human body to control information about the product, seeing variations and viewing items at full size.

User Error

User error deals with the concept of a user making a mistake that stops him from reacting to his intended goal in a computer-related experience. It's the designer's goal to make the errors impossible, but if that is not possible, then the system should have ways for it to self-correct the user's path. There needs to be a balance; if there are too many safeguards in place, it may hinder the experience and cause more harm than help.

Error Systems [1]

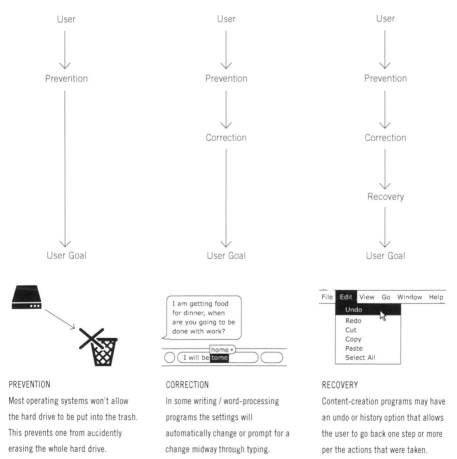

PREVENTION

Most operating systems won't allow the hard drive to be put into the trash. This prevents one from accidently erasing the whole hard drive.

CORRECTION

In some writing / word-processing programs the settings will automatically change or prompt for a change midway through typing.

RECOVERY

Content-creation programs may have an undo or history option that allows the user to go back one step or more per the actions that were taken.

1 The Elements of User Experience: User-Centered Design for the Web and Beyond by Jesse James Garrett p

Variable Narrative Forms

Due to the interactive nature of video games, the typical narrative structure needs to represent multiple paths and decisions. The center core of the narrative form allows the narrative to hold together even though it may need to change during the course of the experience. In the bottom example, the game interaction has four paths—others might have more or less, this is just one of many examples.

Standard Linear Narrative

Variable Narrative Form

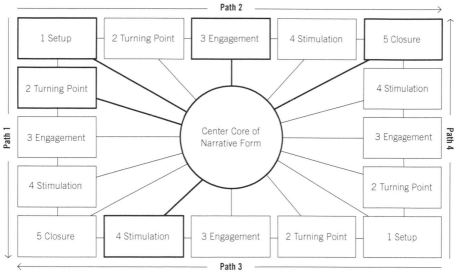

Wearable Computing

Wearable computing (sometimes called smart clothing) is when computer technology is integrated seamlessly into clothing and objects that are worn, and in some cases is just as fashionable as normal clothing wear. Much different from mobile devices that are carried or held, wearable computing is tied directly into the object being worn and go beyond a basic accessory.

Wearable Computing in Glasses

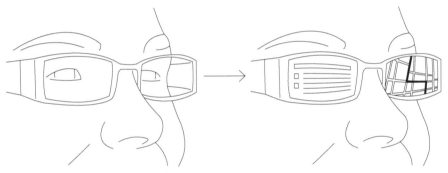

Glasses may be able to switch from their normal function (left) to a mini digital screen (right) based on voice command, giving us directions, vital information and emergency routes when needed.

Gaming Wearable

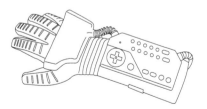

In 1989, Nintendo's Power Glove was an early attempt at wearable computing, combining a glove and game controller into one.

Wearables in Movies

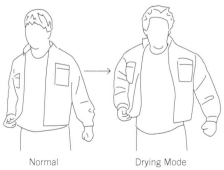

Normal   Drying Mode

In the movie *Back to the Future Part II* a futuristic jacket was able to detect when the wearer was wet and automatically self-dried them.

Wireframes

Wireframes are essentially prototypes of Web sites, applications or digital device interfaces. They act as a blueprint for content structure and sometimes describe functionality. In most cases wireframes do not have any styling or finalized visual design elements. By creating wireframes before the design stage, the stakeholders can focus on content hierarchy, make quicker iterations in content placement and validate various ideas.

Basic Wireframe / Standard Components

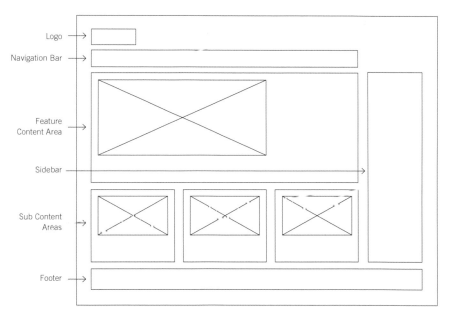

Basic wireframes will show navigational elements, content areas and image placement without stylized details. Each section should have a label describing what it is.

Wireframes with Annotations

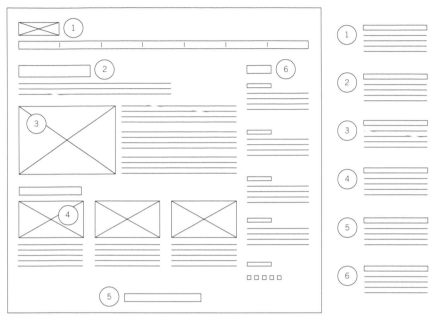

While not always needed, annotations are short descriptions
of functionality and details that need to be communicated
beyond the information presented on the wireframes.

Wireframe Variation

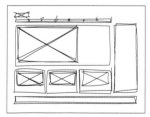

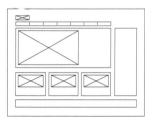

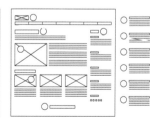

LOW FIDELITY
Sketching with pencil
allows for quicker ideation.

BASIC WIREFRAME
They are usually developed on the
computer and show regional areas
of content and navigation elements.

DETAIL FUNCTIONALITY
More advanced wireframes show
more details and functionality
through the use of annotation.

REFERENCES

Allen, Patrick. 2009. *Quick Query: Dr. BJ Fogg on Fogg Behavior Model*. Practical Ecommerce.<http://www.practicalecommerce.com/articles/1458-Quick-Query-Dr-BJ-Fogg-on-Fogg-Behavior-Model>.

Alexander, Christopher. 1977. *A Pattern Language*. Oxford University Press.

Alvin, Toffler. 1984. *Future Shock*. Bantam.

Apple.com. *Multi-Touch gestures Be more hands-on with your Mac*. <http://www.apple.com/macosx/whats-new/gestures.html>, accessed June 2012.

Block, Bruce. 2007. *The Visual Story, Second Edition: Creating the Visual Structure of Film, TV and Digital Media*. Focal Press 2 edition.

Bilash, Olenka. 2009. *Cognitive Capacity and Cognitive Load*. <http://www2.education.ualberta.ca/staff/olenka.Bilash/best%20of%20bilash/cognitive%20capacity.html>.

Boag, Paul. *Design: 10 techniques for an effective 'call to action,'* < http://boagworld.com/design/10-techniques-for-an-effective-call-to-action/>.

Bowers, John. 2008. *Introduction to Two-Dimensional Design: Understanding Form and Function*. Wiley.

Bozarth, Jane. 2010. *Nuts and Bolts: Brain Bandwidth - Cognitive Load Theory and Instructional Design*. <http://www.learningsolutionsmag.com/articles/498/nuts-and-bolts-brain-bandwidth---cognitive-load-theory-and-instructional-design>.

Breeze, James. 2009. *You look where they look*. <http://usableworld.com.au/2009/03/16/you-look-where-they-look/>.

Caddick, Richard. 2011. *Communicating the User Experience: A Practical Guide for Creating Useful UX Documentation*. Wiley.

Chapman, Cameron. 2009. *"Call To Action" Buttons: Guidelines, Best Practices And Examples*. < http://www.hongkiat.com/blog/call-to-action-buttons-guidelines-best-practices-and-examples/>.

Copper, Alan. 2007. *About Face 3: The Essentials of Interaction Design*. Wiley; 3rd edition.

Cotton, Bob. 1995. *The Cyberspace Lexicon*. Phaidon Press.

Creswell, John. 2008. *Research Design: Qualitative, Quantitative, and Mixed Methods Approaches*. Sage Publications.

Csikszentmihalyi, Mihaly. 1990. *Flow – the Psychology of Optimal Experience*. Harper Perennial.

Design Reviver. 2010. *Designing for a Responsive Web with Heuristic Methods*. <http://designreviver.com/articles/designing-for-a-responsive-web-with-heuristic-methods/>.

Fogg, BJ. 2009. *A Behavior Model for Persuasive Design*. <http://bjfogg.com/fbm_files/page4_1.pdf>.

Fullerton, Tracy. 2008. *Game Design Workshop, Second Edition: A Playcentric Approach to Creating Innovative Games 2 edition*. Morgan Kaufmann.

Gamification Wiki. <http://gamification.org/>.

Garrett, Jesse. 2002. *The Elements of User Experience: User-Centered Design for the Web.* New Riders Press.

Grop, Trevor. 2007. *Design for Emotion and Flow.* <http://www.boxesandarrows.com/view/design-for-emotion >.

Golombisky, Kim. 2010. *White Space is Not Your Enemy: A Beginner's Guide to Communicating Visually through Graphic, Web and Multimedia Design.* Focal Press; 1 edition.

Goodwin, Kim. 2009. *Designing for the Digital Age: How to Create Human-Centered Products and Services.* Wiley.

Goto, Kelly. 2000. *Web Design Workflow.* <www.gotomedia.com/downloads/goto_workflow.pdf>.

Greenfield, Adam. 2006. *Everyware: The Dawning Age of Ubiquitous Computing.* New Riders Publishing.

Halvorson, Kristina. 2009. *Content Strategy for the Web.* New Riders Press.

Hick. 2008. *On the rate of gain of information.* Quarterly Journal of Experimental Psychology Volume 4, Issue 1, 1952.

Horton, William. 1994. *The Icon Book: Visual Symbols for Computer Systems and Documentation.* Wiley.

Iyengar, Shena S. and Mark R. Lepper. 2000. *When choice is demotivating: Can one desire too much of a good thing?.* Journal of Personality and Social Psychology.79:995-1006.

Joiner Associates, 1995. *Flowcharts: Plain & Simple: Learning & Application Guide.* Oriel Inc.

Jones, Brandon. 2010. *Designing Effective Entry Points in Web Design.* <http://webdesign.tutsplus.com/articles/design-theory/designing-effective-entry-points-in-web-design/>.

Jones, Colleen. 2010. *Clout: The Art and Science of Influential Web Content.* New Riders Press.

Jones, Natalie. 2011. *Mental Models: An Interdisciplinary Synthesis of Theory and Methods.* <http://www.ecologyandsociety.org/vol16/iss1/art46/>.

Katz, Steven. 1991. *Film Directing Shot by Shot: Visualizing from Concept to Screen (Michael Wiese Productions.* Michael Wiese.

Krasner, Jon. 2008. *Motion Graphic Design: Applied History and Aesthetics.* Focal Press.

Kuniavsky, Mike. 2010. *Smart Things: Ubiquitous Computing User Experience Design.* Morgan Kaufmann.

Krug, Steve. 2006. *Don't Make Me Think: A Common Sense Approach to Web Usability, 2nd Edition.* PeachPit Press.

Kunz, Willi. 2000. *Typography: Macro and Microaesthetics.* Arthur Niggli; Rev., Expanded Ed.

Lynch, Patrick. 2009. *Web Style Guide, 3rd edition: Basic Design Principles for Creating Web Sites.* Yale University Press.

Mann, Steve. 2002. *Mediated Reality with implementations for everyday life.* Presence Connect, MIT Press journal.

Manuel, Castells. 2009. *The Rise of the Network Society: The Information Age: Economy, Society, and Culture Volume I.* Wiley-Blackwell.

Marcotte, Ethan. 2010. *Responsive Web Design.* <http://www.alistapart.com/articles/responsive-web-design/>.

McCloud, Scott. 1994. *Understanding Comics: The Invisible Art.* William Morrow Paperbacks.

McCloud, Scott. 2000. *Reinventing Comics: How Imagination and Technology Are Revolutionizing an Art Form.* William Morrow Paperbacks.

McLuhan, Marshall. 1995. *Understanding media.* MIT Press.

Miller, Brian. 2012. *Creating a Good User Experience.* <http://www.howinteractivedesign.com/technology/creating-a-good-user-experience>.

Miller, Brian. 2011. *Above the Fold: Understanding the Principles of Successful Web Site Design.* HOW books.

Miller, Carolyn. 2004. *Digital Storytelling: A Creator's Guide to Interactive Entertainment.* Focal Press.

Miller, G. A. 1956. *"The magical number seven, plus or minus two: Some limits on our capacity for processing information."* The Psychological Review, 1956, vol. 63, pp. 81-97.

Moggridge, Bill. 2007. *Designing Interactions.* MIT Press.

Murry, Janet. 2011. *Inventing the Medium: Principles of Interaction Design as a Cultural Practice.* The MIT Press.

Nielsen, Jakob. 2012. <UseIt.com>.

Nielsen, Jakob. 1999. *Designing Web Usability.* Peachpit Press.

Nielsen, Jakob. 2009. *Eyetracking Web Usability.* New Riders Press.

Nielsen, Jakob. 2007. *Breadcrumb Navigation Increasingly Useful.* <http://www.useit.com/alertbox/breadcrumbs.html>.

Norman, Donald. 1989. *The Psychology of Everyday Things.* Basic Books.

O'Grady, Jenn. 2008. *The Information Design Handbook,* HOW Books.

Plass, Jan. 2010. *Cognitive Load Theory.* Cambridge University Press.

Quinn, Sara. 2007. *Eyetracking the News.* The Poynter Institute.

Redish, Janice. 2007. *Letting Go of the Words: Writing Web Content that Works (Interactive Technologies.* Morgan Kaufmann.

Reimann, Robert. 2005. *Personas, Scenarios, and Emotion Design.* New Riders Press.

Rigie, Mitchell. 2010. *The Power of Divergent and Convergent Thinking: Guide Your Group's Thinking Process to New Heights of Productivity.* <http://smartstorming-blog.com/the-power-of-divergent-and-convergent-thinkingguide-your-groups-thinking-process-to-new-heights-of-productivity/>.

Saffer, Dan. 2008. *Designing Gestural Interfaces: Touchscreens and Interactive Devices.* O'Reilly Media.

Saffer, Dan. 2010. *Designing for Interaction: Creating Innovative Applications and Devices (2nd Edition).* Peachpit Press.

Salen, Katie and Eric Zimmerman. 2003. *Rules of Play: Game Design Fundamentals.* MIT Press.

Samara, Timothy. 2005. *Making and Breaking the Grid: A Graphic Design Layout Workshop.* Rockport Publishers.

Shneiderman, Ben. 1986. *Designing the User Interface: Strategies for Effective Human-Computer Interaction.* Addison Wesley.

Spencer, Donna. 2004. *Card sorting: a definitive guide.* <http://www.boxesandarrows.com/view/card_sorting_a_definitive_guide>.

Thompson, Clive. 2012. *Clive Thompson on Analog Designs in the Digital Age.* <http://www.wired.com/magazine/2012/01/st_thompson_analog/>.

Tidwell, Jennifer. 2006. *Designing Interfaces: Patterns for Effective Interaction Design.* O'Reilly Media.

Tuck, Michael. 2010. *Going with the Flow.* <http://www.iraqtimeline.com/maxdesign/basicdesign/principles/prinfloat.html>.

Tufte, Edward. 1983. *The Visual Display of Quantitative Information.* Graphic Press.

Unger, Russ. 1990. *A Project Guide to UX Design: For user experience designers in the field or in the making.* New Riders Press.

Veen, Jeffrey. 2002. *Doing a Content Inventory (Or, A Mind-Numbingly Detailed Odyssey Through Your Web Site).* <http://www.adaptivepath.com/ideas/doing-content-inventory>.

VideoMcluhan.com. *Hot and Cool Media.* <http://www.videomcluhan.com/hotandcool.html>.

Weinschenk, Susan. 2011. *100 Things Every Designer needs to know about people.* New Riders Press.

Wotel, Paul. *Analog. Digital. What's the Difference.?* <http://telecom.hellodirect.com/docs/Tutorials/AnalogVsDigital.1.051501.asp>.

IMAGE CREDITS

"Laptop" symbol on page 20 is by The Noun Project from thenounproject.com collection.

"iPad" symbol on page 20 is by The Noun Project from thenounproject.com collection.

"iPhone" symbol on page 20 is by The Noun Project from thenounproject.com collection.

"Drop" symbol on page 27 is by Nithin Davis Nanthikkara from thenounproject.com collection.

"Error" symbol on page 28 is by Anas Ramadan from thenounproject.com collection.

"Power" symbol on page 37 is Public Domain.

"Moon" symbol on page 43 is by Travis Yunis from thenounproject.com collection.

"Fast Food" symbol on page 43 is by Saman Bemel-Benrud from thenounproject.com collection.

"Plant" symbol on page 43 is by RD Granados from thenounproject.com collection.

"Smile" symbol on page 43 is by Rob Schill from thenounproject.com collection.

"Ribbon" symbol on page 43 is by Nicolò Bertoncin from thenounproject.com collection.

"Coupon" symbol on page 43 is by Nathan Thomson from thenounproject.com collection.

"Bicycle" symbol on page 44 is by Public Domain.

"Light Bulb" symbol on page 78 is by Ben Rex Furneaux from thenounproject.com collection.

"Hard Drive" symbol on page 80 is by The Noun Project from thenounproject.com collection.

"Trash Can" symbol on page 80 is by John Caserta from thenounproject.com collection.

pg. 24. The Data-Ink Ratio Illustration reference. <http://www.tbray.org/ongoing/data-ink/di1> by Tim Bray.

pg. 25. Decision Scale Diagram. *Game Design Workshop, A Playcentric Approach to Creating Innovative Games* by Tracy Fullerton.

pg. 40. Flow State Diagram. *Anxiety, Boredom and Flow* (Csikszentmihalyi, 1990) (captions added van Gorp, 2006).

pg. 42. Fogg Behavior Model. <http://www.behaviormodel.org/>.

pg. 51. Interface Design Hub and Spoke. *Designing Interfaces: Patterns for Effective Interaction Design* by Jenifer Tidwell.

pg. 57. Alignment Diagram of Mental Model. *Mental Models: Aligning Design Strategy with Human Behavior* by Indi Young.

pg. 59. Multi-Touch Gestures. *Designing Gestural Interfaces: Touchscreens and Interactive Devices* by Dan Saffer.

pg. 69. Digital Scanning Experience Diagram. *Don't Make Me Think: A Common Sense Approach to Web Usability* by Steve Krug.

pg. 82. *Nintendo's Power Glove.* Copyright Nintendo Inc.

pg. 82. *Back to the Future Part II.* Copyright Universal Pictures.

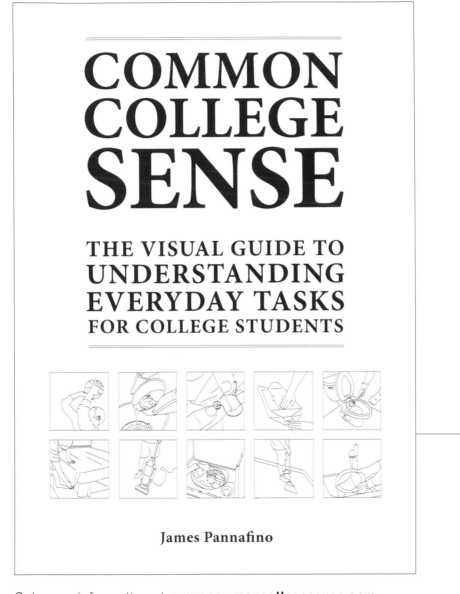

Get more information at: **www.commoncollegesense.com**

Ask your library or bookstore to order: ISBN-13: 978-0982634806

Or purchase directly from www.amazon.com today!

A quick look at Common College Sense

When young people go to college, they are expected to gain the knowledge to survive and thrive in their professional fields. But what about the common-sense knowledge that is needed to accomplish common daily tasks not typically taught in college? Tasks like tying a tie, changing a tire, or properly cleaning the kitchen. This book uses both visual diagrams and written explanations to clearly describe each common-sense task.

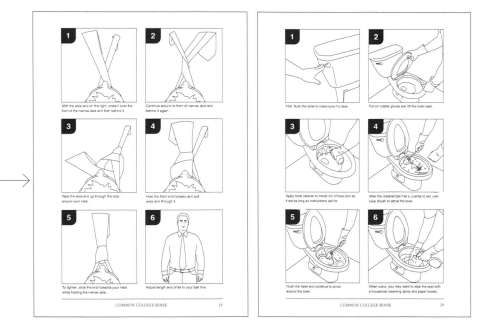

Common College Sense is a great book for high-school graduates, college students, and young people entering the real world. It also makes a perfect gift for birthdays, holidays, and graduations.